You Shall Not Want

Titles in the *Thirty Days with a Great Spiritual Teacher* series

ALL WILL BE WELL
Based on the Classic Spirituality of *Julian of Norwich*

GOD AWAITS YOU
Based on the Classic Spirituality of *Meister Eckhart*

LET NOTHING DISTURB YOU
A Journey to the Center of the Soul with *Teresa of Avila*

PEACE OF HEART
Based on the Life and Teachings of *Francis of Assisi*

TRUE SERENITY
Based on Thomas A Kempis' *The Imitation of Christ*

YOU SHALL NOT WANT
A Spiritual Journey Based on *The Psalms*

Future titles in the series will focus on authors and classic works such as
Hildegaard of Bingen, John of the Cross, The Cloud of Unknowing, Augustine,
Catherine of Sienna, Brother Lawrence, and others.

YOU SHALL NOT WANT

A Spiritual Journey Based on

The Psalms

Richard Chilson, C.S.P.

AVE MARIA PRESS Notre Dame, Indiana 46556

Richard Chilson is the author of over a dozen books on Catholicism and world religions. He currently serves as a chaplain at the University of California at Berkeley.

The psalms included in this book are paraphrased from the King James Version of the Bible. Very often passages from various psalms have been gathered together based on a similarity in their themes.

Copyright © 1996 Quest Associates.

International Standard Book Number: 0-87793-571-8
Library of Congress Catalog Card Number: 95-80889
Cover and text design by Elizabeth J. French
Printed and bound in the United States of America.

Contents

Behold, how good and pleasant it is
when people dwell in unity!
It is like the precious oil upon the head,
running down upon the beard,
upon the beard of Aaron,
running down on the collar of his robes.
It is like the dew of Hermon,
which falls on the mountains of Zion.
For there the Lord has commanded the blessing,
life forevermore.

—Psalm 133

The Psalms

The Bible's book of psalms is a collection of prayers and hymns from the Israelite tradition, which Jews and Christians still share as their common prayer. These words and themes have shaped prayer in the West.

The psalms were gathered from private prayers and public liturgies. There are several major types, including hymns, entreaties, thanksgiving psalms, and penitential psalms. The hymns invite us to praise the Lord. They give reasons why God deserves such praise. They may point to the glory and beauty of creation or remember God's saving acts in Israelite history. The entreaties are spoken directly to God and ask for something. An individual or a whole people may be in trouble, surrounded by enemies, slandered, threatened with war. Or, the prayer might be penitential, a confession of sin asking God's forgiveness. Psalms of entreaty and penitential psalms often conclude with confidence that God will respond favorably. The psalms of thanksgiving thank God for rescue, for favors. Again, they may be the prayers of an individual or of a people.

Because these prayers are over two thousand years old, we can expect some difficulty making them our own today. Certain themes and images stand in our way. Most graphic is an image asking that the children of enemies have their heads dashed against a rock. Such a sentiment might have been acceptable when the psalm was written but is not today.

The language itself forms another obstacle. The psalms come out of a patriarchal culture and reflect it. This paraphrase is grounded in the King James tradition, because that translation has been paramount in the English language; its phrases have entered our literature and vernacular speech. But we have reworked the language spoken both of and to God to make it gender neutral and to see that no one gender dominates. Finally, we have updated archaic words and expressions.

A third obstacle may be failing to understand that although the psalms arose within a specific religious and historical moment, their appropriateness as prayer is not confined to that time and space. The nation Israel, for example, was born through a rebellion of slaves fleeing Egypt into the Sinai peninsula. They believed their escape was made possible by their God through their leader Moses. The escape climaxed at the shores of the Red Sea. Pharaoh's army was in hot pursuit. But at the final moment Moses stretched forth his arm and God parted the sea so that the slaves could flee over dry ground. When the Egyptians' chariots followed them the sea returned to its bed and the Egyptians were drowned.

In praying the psalms we need not be bound by the original meaning. Where the psalm speaks of the Red Sea, we might substitute other acts of salvation from our own traditional or personal history. Such a practice is quite within the original tradition of reading the Bible.

The psalms are a living tradition by which succeeding generations may interpret their own experience. Americans can look back at the coming of the pilgrims as a recurrence of that original Exodus. These persecuted people also fled across the waters to a new beginning. African-Americans have made these images their own, and the Exodus has inspired their journey from slavery to freedom, a journey that continues to this day.

Awareness of other biblical moments and themes is also helpful in praying the psalms today. For example, we can reflect upon the law or concept of kingship or even a place such as Zion.

After fleeing Egypt Moses led Israel into the wilderness. There God gave the Law by which Israel was to live. The people entered into a covenant with God, who agreed to protect them and make them prosper. The people in turn agreed to abide by the law. In the psalms the law symbolizes God's ways, which lead to life.

Later in the history of Israel, charismatic leaders gave way to kings. The ideal figure of the king is David, a shepherd who led Israel to her moment of greatness. Kingship may prove another difficulty for the modern reader. In the ancient world the king was a sacred figure who embodied the people's welfare. King and people were linked together; when one sinned or suffered the other did also. Perhaps we might see the king as a symbol for a higher power.

Other images cluster around the king. Although Israel's greatness was short-lived, the idea of the great king grew in her memory and flowered as the Messiah, the one who would restore her glory and freedom. As Israel declined in greatness and eventually was driven into exile, Jerusalem, David's capital, became the image of the "holy city." Salem means "peace," and Jerusalem came to represent the ideal peaceful city. The mountain upon which the Temple was built, Zion, now evokes a future coming together of the world's peoples in peace.

Seeing the psalms as the prayers of a people, rather than of an individual, can help us make them our own. We may not feel especially grateful when praying a psalm of thanksgiving or in trouble when praying a psalm asking for rescue. But entering these psalms as the prayers of God's people, of whom we are a part, we pray on behalf of the entire people. Someone is suffering somewhere; others are thankful. Our world today is plagued by sickness, poverty, and oppression; our streets are filled with crime and violence. We may try to shield ourselves from such evil, but we are part of this society and a spiritual person identifies with the suffering in the hope of alleviating pain and allowing all to share in God's blessings. The psalms help us unite humanity and dissolve boundaries. This use of the psalms expands awareness and increases compassion.

Sin is proclaimed by the media constantly. On a spiritual path the first step is to acknowledge our condition and our role in creating sinful structures. In addition we sin personally. We carry grudges and resentments. We support structures of oppression and violence. The way out of such misery is through honest confession, asking God's healing and forgiveness. The penitential psalms confess sins and ask God's forgiveness. We pray them not only for ourselves but for our society and world.

All of these themes are found in the selection of psalms chosen to accompany you on this thirty-day spiritual journey. You will, we hope, find in them the same nourishment enjoyed by seekers ever since they were first prayed so many generations ago.

How to Pray This Book

The purpose of this book is to open a gate for you, to make accessible the spiritual experience and wisdom of one of the world's great collections of prayers, the psalms.

In using this book, however, keep in mind that these are first and foremost prayers. The psalms do not teach methods of spirituality. They are examples of how to pray. As you move through the book, pray them aloud; they are first of all oral literature. They were chanted and sung in public long before they were read in private. They are poetry rather than prose, so dwell upon the images, the words used, the feelings evoked. If a particular word or phrase appeals to you as you pray, stay with it. Ruminate upon it. It is not necessary to finish reading the psalm. The psalms are not content but rather vehicles to raise our hearts toward God.

This, then, is not a book for mere reading. It invites you to meditate and pray its words on a daily basis over a period of thirty days.

It is a handbook for a spiritual journey.

Before you read the "rules" for taking this spiritual journey, remember that this book is meant to free your spirit, not confine it. If on any day the meditation does not resonate well for you, turn elsewhere to find a passage which seems to best fit the spirit of your day and your soul. Don't hesitate to repeat a day as often as you like until you feel that you have discovered what the Spirit, through the words of the author, has to say to your spirit.

Here are suggestions on how to use this book as a cornerstone of your prayers.

As Your Day Begins

As the day begins set aside a quiet moment in a quiet place to read the psalm suggested for the day

. The passage is short, never more than a couple of hundred words. It may combine verses selected from more than one psalm in order to give a spiritual focus, a spiritual center to your whole day. It is designed to remind you as another day begins of your own existence at a spiritual level. But most of all the purpose of the passage is to remind you that at this moment and at every moment during your day you will be living and acting in the divine presence, that you are invited continually, but quietly to live in and through God.

A word of advice: read slowly. Very slowly. Read aloud, if you can. Listen to the poetry. Visualize the images. Don't read to get to the end, but to savor each part of the meditation. You never know what short phrase or word will trigger a response in your spirit. Give the words a chance. After all, you are not just reading this passage, you are praying it. Here is your chance to establish a mood of serenity that will color your whole day. There is no hurry.

All Through Your Day

Immediately following the day's reading you will find a single sentence or phrase from the psalm passage. We suggest you use it as a mantra. This phrase is meant as a companion for your spirit as it moves through a busy day. Write it on a 3" x 5" card or on the appropriate page of your day book. Look at it as often as you can, Repeat it quietly to yourself and go your way.

It is not meant to stop you in your tracks or to distract you from responsibilities but simply, gently, to remind you of the presence of God and your desire to respond to this presence.

As Your Day Is Ending

This is a time for letting go of the day.

Find a quiet place and quiet your spirit. Breathe deeply. Inhale and exhale—slowly and deliberately, again and again, until you feel your body let go of its tension.

Now read the questions that are presented for you as a way of reviewing your day in the light of the meditation. Answer them slowly, thoughtfully, without anxiety or stress. They are not a test but simply a way of concentrating the spiritual energy of your day as it comes to an end.

When you are ready, read the evening prayer slowly, phrase by phrase. You will find phrases to remind you of the meditation with which you began the day and the mantra that has accompanied you all through your day.

It is a time for summary and closure.

Invite God to embrace you with love and to protect you through the night.

Sleep well.

Some Other Ways to Use This Book

1. Use it any way your spirit leads you. As suggested earlier, skip a passage that doesn't resonate for you on a given day, or repeat for a second day or even several days a passage whose richness speaks to your spirit.

2. Take two passages and/or their mantras—the more contrasting

the better—and spend time discovering how their similarities or differences illumine your path.

3. Start a spiritual journal to record and deepen your experience of this thirty-day journey. Using either the mantra or another phrase from the psalm that appeals to you, write a spiritual account of your day or a spiritual reflection. Compose your own "psalm."

4. Join the millions who are seeking to deepen their spiritual life by joining with others to form small groups. More and more people are doing this to aid and support each other in their mutual spiritual quest. Meet once a week, or at least every other week, to discuss and pray one of the psalms. There are many books and guides available to help you make such a group effective.

Thirty Days with
The Psalms

Day One

◆◆◆◆◆

My Day Begins

The heavens proclaim the glory of God;
and the firmament discloses the divine handiwork.
Day to day they pour forth speech,
and night to night speak knowledge.
There is no speech, nor are there words;
their voice is not heard;
yet their voice goes out through all the earth,
and their words to the end of the world.

In them God has set a tent for the sun,
which comes forth like a bridegroom from his chamber,
and like a strong man runs its course with joy.
Its rising is from the end of the heavens,
and its circuit to the end of them;
there is nothing hidden from its heat.
The Law of the Lord is perfect;
it restores the soul.
The testimony of the Lord is sure;
it makes simple people wise.
The ordinances of the Lord are true
and altogether right.
More to be desired are they than gold,
even much fine gold,
sweeter also than honey

and drippings of the honeycomb.
Let the words of my mouth
and the meditation of my heart
be acceptable in your sight,
O Lord, my rock and my redeemer.

All Through the Day

The heavens proclaim the glory of God.

My Day Is Ending

Take a few minutes to relax
and look back over your day.

Where did you discover God's glory
in creation today?

Spend some time remembering
how you experienced nature today.

Night Prayer

Wondrous Lord,
let me thank you
for this beautiful earth.
I see you in the heavens,
in the plants and animals,
and in other people.
Let me acknowledge
and greet you in all these things.

Day Two

❖❖❖❖❖

My Day Begins

God chose his servant David,
and took him from the sheepfolds;
from tending the nursing ewes God brought him
to shepherd God's people,
Israel, his inheritance.

With upright heart he tended them
and guided them with skillful hand.

The Lord is my shepherd, I shall not want;

I lie down in green pastures.
God leads me beside restful waters,
restoring my soul.
I walk the way of truth
for the sake of God's name.
Even though I walk through
the valley of the shadow of death,
I fear no evil,
for you are with me;
your rod and staff
give me comfort.
You set a table before me
in the presence of my enemies;
you anoint my head with oil,
and my cup overflows.

Surely goodness and mercy shall follow me
all my life long;
and I shall dwell in the Lord's house
forever.

◆◆◆◆◆

All Through the Day

I shall dwell in the Lord's house
forever.

◆◆◆◆◆

My Day Is Ending

Take a moment or two to relax.
Breathe slowly and deeply a few times.

When you are centered,
re-read today's selection,
pausing with the images that
appeal to you.

Night Prayer

I give my life to your safekeeping,
Lord.
I trust in your care.
Thank you for the many
gifts you have given me.
Let me dwell with you
all my days.

Day Three

◆◆◆◆◆

My Day Begins

I lift up my eyes to the hills.
Whence comes my help?
My help comes from the Lord,
who made heaven and earth.
God will not let my foot be moved,
and will not slumber caring for us.

Behold, God who keeps Israel
will neither slumber nor sleep.
The Lord is our keeper,
our shade on our right hand.
The sun shall not hurt us by day,
nor the moon by night.
The Lord will preserve us from all evil.

God will keep our life.
The Lord will keep
our going and coming
from this time forth and forevermore.

We lift up our eyes to you,
Lord of the heavens and earth!
Behold, as the eyes of servants
look to the hand of their master,

as the eyes of a maid
to the hand of her mistress,
so our eyes look to the Lord our God,
who shows us mercy.

All Through the Day

My help comes from the Lord
who made heaven and earth.

YOU SHALL NOT WANT

My Day Is Ending

Was there a time today
when you asked for God's help?
A time when you could have
asked for help but didn't?

Spend a few minutes with the image of
God as your protector and refuge.
How do you relate to such an image?

Night Prayer

God, my help and my hope,
I give myself into your care.
I trust that you will guide
my life for the best.
May your mercy
be upon your servants
forever.

Day Four

My Day Begins

I call upon you, O Lord; hasten to me.

Give ear to my voice when I call to you.
Let my prayers rise like incense before you,
and the lifting up of my hands
be as an evening sacrifice.

Set a guard over my mouth, O Lord;
keep watch over the door of my lips.
Incline my heart away from any evil,

from busying myself with wicked deeds
in the company of evildoers.
Let them not be my companions.

Let a good person rebuke me in kindness,
but let the oil of the wicked never anoint my head.

Answer me, O Lord,
for your faithful love is good;
according to your abundant mercy, turn to me.
Do not hide your face from your servant,
for I am in distress; hasten to answer me.
For the Lord hears the needy
and does not despise those who are in bonds.

Let heaven and earth praise God,
the seas, and everything that moves therein.

YOU SHALL NOT WANT

For God will save Zion
and rebuild the cities of Judah;
God's servants shall dwell there and possess it;
their children shall inherit it,
and those who love God's name shall dwell in it.

All Through the Day

Let my prayers rise like incense
before you.

My Day Is Ending

Light a candle and burn some incense
as a mindful prayer.
Spend a few moments
gazing at the smoke rising from the incense,
imagining that it is your prayer.

(If you do not have the objects at hand,
imagine the scene.)

Night Prayer

Gracious God,
thank you for leading me
through this day.
Keep me always in your good favor,
and let me share in the
inheritance you have prepared
for your friends.

Day Five

◆◆◆◆◆

My Day Begins

As a deer longs for flowing streams,
so my soul longs for you, my God.
My soul thirsts for God, for the living God.
When shall I come and behold
the face of God?
My tears have been my food day and night,
while people constantly taunt me,
"Where is your God?"

These things I remember, as I pour out my soul:
How I went with the throng,
and led them in procession to the house of God
with glad shouts and songs of thanksgiving,
a multitude keeping festival.
Why are you cast down, O my soul,
and why are you disquieted within me?
Hope in God, for I shall again praise
my help and my God.
My soul is cast down within me,
therefore I remember you
from the land of Jordan.
Deep calls to deep
at the thunder of your cataracts;
all your waves and billows

have gone over me.
By day the Lord shows forth steadfast love,
and at night God's song is with me,
a prayer to the God of my life.
Why are you cast down, O my soul,
and why are you disquieted within me?
Hope in God, for I shall again sing praises to
my help and my God.

All Through the Day

My soul thirsts for the living God.

My Day Is Ending

Take a few minutes to relax.
Follow your breathing
and let go of your thoughts.

Reflect on this phrase from today's psalm:
"At night God's song is with me."

Remain with the phrase.
Let it repeat itself in your mind;
let it evoke feelings and images.

Night Prayer

Lord, I hunger for you.
I thirst for you,
like the deer for living water.
Show me you are with me,
even when I feel far removed
from your presence.
Teach me patience
and to trust in your love.

Day Six

●◆●◆●◆●

My Day Begins

Bless the Lord, O my soul;
all that is within me, bless God's holy name.
Do not forget all God's benefits,
who forgives all your iniquities,
who heals all your diseases,
who redeems your life from the pit,
who crowns you with steadfast love and mercy,
who satisfies you with good as long as you live,

so that your youth is renewed like the eagle's.
The Lord works vindication
and justice for all who are oppressed.
The Lord is merciful and gracious,
slow to anger and abounding in steadfast love.
God does not deal with us according to our sins,
nor requite us according to our iniquities.
For as the heavens are high above the earth,
so great is God's steadfast love
toward those who love him;
as far as the east is from the west,
so far does God remove our transgressions from us.
As for us, our days are like grass.
We flourish like a flower of the field;
the wind passes over it, and it is gone,

and its place knows it no more.
But the steadfast love of the Lord
is from everlasting to everlasting
upon those who are faithful.
Bless the Lord, all creation,
God's friends who do the Lord's will.
Bless the Lord, O my soul!

All Through the Day

The Lord is merciful and gracious.

My Day Is Ending

Take a few minutes to relax
and let go of the day.

Now reread the psalm.
Pick a line that speaks to you
and spend a few minutes
reflecting upon that line.
How does it relate to your situation today?

Night Prayer

Loving God,
I praise you and thank you
for all you have done for me.
I turn to you for help, and you are there,
I turn to you for forgiveness,
and you assure me of your love.
I bless you with all my being
and praise your wondrous acts
of kindness.

Day Seven

❖❖❖❖❖

My Day Begins

In Judah God is known;
God's name is great in Israel.
God abides in Salem,
and dwells in Zion.
There God broke the flashing arrows,
the shield, the sword, and the weapons of war.
Glorious are you, more majestic
than the everlasting mountains.

The stout-hearted were stripped of their spoils;
they sank into sleep;
all the warriors
were unable to use their hands.
At your rebuke, O God of Jacob and Rachel,
both rider and horse lay stunned.
But you are most awesome!
Who can stand before you
when once your anger is roused?
From the heavens you announced judgment;
the earth feared and was quiet
when God arose to save the oppressed of the earth.
Make your vows to the Lord your God;
let those from all around bring gifts.
On the holy mount stands the city God founded;

the Lord loves the gates of Zion
more than all the dwelling places on earth.
Glorious things are spoken of you,
O city of God.
The Lord records the peoples,
"This one was born there."
Singers and dancers alike say,
"All my springs are in you."

All Through the Day

Make your vows to the Lord your God;
let those from all around bring gifts.

My Day Is Ending

Two images are prominent in this psalm:
war and the city.
Spend some time tonight
reflecting upon both.

How does conflict appear in your life today?
How do you rely upon God in such conflict?
How do you associate God with the city?
Is the city a holy place for you?
How can it become more God's city?

Night Prayer

Lord, I praise you
wherever I am in my life,
in whatever struggles
I am going through.
Help me to sense your presence,
and celebrate you there.

Day Eight

◆◆◆◆◆

My Day Begins

Oh, give thanks to the Lord, for God is good;
God's steadfast love endures forever.
Oh, give thanks to the God of gods,
for God's steadfast love endures forever.
Oh, give thanks to the Lord of lords,
for God's steadfast love endures forever;
to the One who alone does great wonders,
for God's steadfast love endures forever;

to the One who by understanding made the heavens,
for God's steadfast love endures forever;
to the One who spread earth out upon the waters,
for God's steadfast love endures forever;
to the One who made the great lights,
for God's steadfast love endures forever;
the sun to rule over the day,
for God's steadfast love endures forever;
the moon and stars to rule over the night,
for God's steadfast love endures forever;
who brought Israel out from Egypt,
for God's steadfast love endures forever;
to the One who divided the Red Sea asunder,
for God's steadfast love endures forever;
and made Israel pass through the midst of it,

for God's steadfast love endures forever;
to the One who led us through the wilderness,
for God's steadfast love endures forever.
The Lord remembered us in our low estate,
for God's steadfast love endures forever;
the Lord gives food to all flesh,
for God's steadfast love endures forever.
Oh, give thanks to the God of heaven,
for God's steadfast love endures forever.

All Through the Day

God's steadfast love endures forever.

My Day Is Ending

First take a few moments to relax.
Pay attention to your breath,
following it in and out.

Now pray the psalm again aloud
calling to mind
all the ways God's steadfast love
has appeared to you today.

Night Prayer

Lord, your faithful, steadfast love,
sustains and protects me
all my life long.
I am glad to be your servant
and to show you forth to all
in all my experiences,
in my sufferings as well as my joys.

Day Nine

My Day Begins

O Lord, our Lord,
how majestic is your name in all the earth.
Your glory is chanted above the heavens
by the mouths of babes and infants.
You have founded a bulwark because of your foes,
to still the enemy and the avenger.
I look at your heavens, your handiwork,
the moon and the stars you have set up;

what is humankind that you are mindful of us,
and the children of Adam that you care for us?
Yet you have made us little less than God,
and have crowned us with glory and honor.
You have given us dominion
over the works of your hands;
you have put all things under our feet,
all sheep and oxen,
and also the beasts of the field,
the birds of the air, and the fish of the sea,
whatever passes along the paths of the sea.
O Lord, our Lord,
how majestic is your name in all the earth!

O Lord, my heart is not lifted up,
my eyes are not raised too high;

I do not occupy myself with things
too great and too marvelous for me.
But I have calmed and quieted my soul,
as a child is quieted at its mother's breast;
as a child that is quieted is my soul.
O Israel, hope in the Lord
from this time forth and forevermore.

All Through the Day

Who are we
that you are mindful of us?

My Day Is Ending

Take a few moments to settle down.
Take a couple of slow, deep breaths.
Let the day's worries out
as you exhale.

Now slowly pray the last
paragraph of today's psalm.
Pause with each phrase
and enter into it.
Let the images bring you peace.

Night Prayer

Lord, how marvelous are all your works.
Teach us to be in harmony
with all creation;
do not allow us
to consider ourselves
above all other things.
Teach us instead to be
caregivers to all your works.

Day Ten

My Day Begins

By the waters of Babylon,
there we sat down and wept,
when we remembered Zion.
On the willows there we hung up our lyres.
For there our captors required of us songs,
and our tormentors, mirth, saying,
"Sing us one of the songs of Zion!"
How shall we sing the Lord's song

in a foreign land?
If I forget you, O Jerusalem,
let my right hand wither!
Let my tongue cleave to the roof of my mouth,
if I do not remember you, if I do not set Jerusalem
above my highest joy.
I was glad when they said to me,
"Let us go to the house of the Lord."
Our feet have been standing
within your gates, O Jerusalem.
Jerusalem, built as a city, bound firmly together,
to which the tribes go up, the tribes of the Lord,
as was decreed for Israel,
to give thanks to the name of the Lord.
There thrones for judgment were set,

the thrones of the house of David.
Pray for the peace of Jerusalem.
"May they prosper who love you!
Peace be within your walls,
and security within your towers."
For my sisters' and brothers' sake
I will say, "Peace be within you."
For the sake of the house of the Lord our God,
I will seek your good.

All Through the Day

Peace be within you.

My Day Is Ending

Tonight let us focus upon
the theme of exile.
Exiles of various kinds
form part of our lives:
we may be parted from family and friends;
we may feel estranged from a group;
illness makes us feel isolated and cut off.
How have you experienced exile?
Did you sense God's presence in the exile?
How might prayer such as this psalm
lighten the experience of exile?

Night Prayer

Lord, may I find you
and praise you
in the midst of my life in your holy city.
May I be a builder of peace
and security
so that all may enjoy
the wonders of your glory.

Day Eleven

My Day Begins

Have mercy on me, O God,
according to your steadfast love;
according to your abundant mercy
blot out my transgressions.
Wash me thoroughly from my iniquity,
and cleanse me from my sin.
For I know my transgressions,
and my sin is ever before me.

Against you only have I sinned
and done that which is evil in your sight,
so that you are justified in your sentence
and blameless in your judgment.
Behold, I was brought forth in iniquity,
and in sin my mother conceived me.
Behold, you desire truth in the inward being;
therefore teach me wisdom in my secret heart.
Purge me with hyssop, and I shall be clean;
wash me, and I shall be whiter than snow.
Fill me with joy and gladness;
let the bones which you have broken rejoice.
Hide your face from my sins
and blot out all my iniquities.
Create in me a clean heart, O God,

and put a new and right spirit within me.
Restore to me the joy of your salvation
and uphold me with a willing spirit.
Then I will teach transgressors your ways,
and sinners will return to you.
O Lord, open my lips,
and my mouth shall show forth your praise.
The sacrifice acceptable to God is a broken spirit;
a humble and contrite heart you will not spurn.

All Through the Day

Create in me a clean heart, O God.

YOU SHALL NOT WANT

My Day Is Ending

After taking some time to quiet down,
look at your life in terms of sin.
Where have you gone wrong?
Where do you need healing and forgiveness?

Bring your prayer to God now,
confident that God
hears your words and
restores you to life and health.

Night Prayer

Lord, help me to see
and acknowledge my faults and sins.
Give me the strength
to confess them to you
and ask for them to be removed
so that I may serve you
in joy and gladness
and teach others
of your forgiveness and goodness.

Day Twelve

My Day Begins

My heart is steadfast,
O God, my heart is steadfast.
I will sing and make melody.
Awake, my soul!
Awake, O harp and lyre!
I will awake the dawn.

I will give thanks to you, O Lord, among the peoples,
I will sing praises to you among the nations.

For your steadfast love is great above the heavens,
your faithfulness reaches to the clouds.
Be exalted, O God, above the heavens.
Let your glory be over all the earth.
That your beloved may be delivered,
give help by your right hand and answer me.

I give you thanks, O Lord, with my whole heart;
before the powerful I sing your praise;
I bow down toward your holy temple
and give thanks to your name
for your steadfast love and your faithfulness;
for you have exalted above everything
your name and your word.

On the day I called, you answered me,
my strength of soul you increased.

All the powerful of the earth shall praise you, O Lord,
for they have heard the words of your mouth.

All Through the Day

Your steadfast love
is great above the heavens.

My Day Is Ending

Look back over your day.
Where have you praised and thanked God today?
How might you have given praise
and thanksgiving?
How might your day have changed
had you brought more thanksgiving into it?

Night Prayer

Lord, thank you for all things,
for the beauties of your earth,
the majesty of your heavens,
the gift of life and breath
to all creatures,
and for giving me this day
as an opportunity to know you.

Day Thirteen

_____◆◆◆◆◆_____

My Day Begins

I waited patiently for the Lord
who inclined to me and heard my cry.
God drew me up from the desolate pit,
out of the miry bog,
and set my feet upon a rock,
making my steps secure.
God put a new song in my mouth,
a song of praise to our God.
Many will see and fear and trust God.

Blessed is the one who makes the Lord his trust,
who does not turn to the proud.
You have multiplied, O Lord my God,
your wondrous deeds and thoughts toward us;
none can compare with you!
Were I to proclaim and tell of them,
they would be more than can be numbered.
Sacrifice and offering you do not desire;
but you have given me an open ear.
I have told the glad news of deliverance
in the great congregation;
I have not restrained my lips, as you know, O Lord.
I have not hidden your saving help within my heart,
Do not, O Lord, withhold mercy from me.
For evils have encompassed me without number;

my iniquities have overtaken me, till I cannot see;
they are more than the hairs of my head;
my heart fails me.
O Lord, make haste to help me!
As for me, I am poor and needy;
but the Lord takes thought for me.
You are my help and my deliverer;
do not tarry, O my God.

All Through the Day

I wait patiently for the Lord,
who hears my cry.

My Day Is Ending

Take a few minutes in quiet now
to recall some time in your own life
when you were in trouble
and called out to God for help.
How did that aid come to you?
How might you share your story
with others so that they might
know of God's goodness?

Night Prayer

Lord, I turn to you
when I am in distress.
Thank you for being there for me.
I will tell others of your mercy and love
so that all may come to know
your kindness.

Day Fourteen

<hr>

My Day Begins

O God, you are my God, whom I seek,
my soul thirsts for you;
my flesh faints for you,
as in a dry and weary land where no water is.
So I have looked upon you in the sanctuary,
beholding your power and glory.
Because your steadfast love is better than life,
my lips will praise you.

So I will bless you as long as I live;
I will lift up my hands and call on your name.
My mouth praises you with joyful lips,
when I think of you upon my bed,
and meditate on you in the watches of the night;
for you have been my help,
and in the shadow of your wings I sing for joy.
My soul clings to you;
your right hand upholds me.
Teach me your way, O Lord,
that I may walk in your truth.
O God, insolent people have risen up against me;
a ruthless band seeks my life,
and they do not set God before them.
But you, O Lord, are a God merciful and gracious,

slow to anger and abounding
in steadfast love and faithfulness.
Turn to me and take pity on me;
give strength to your servant,
and save the child of your handmaid.
Show me a sign of your favor,
that those who hate me may see
and be put to shame
because you, Lord, have helped and comforted me.

All Through the Day

O God, my soul thirsts for you.

My Day Is Ending

Relax and spend a few minutes
in quiet now.
How have you experienced
God in times of adversity?
How might you depend more upon God?
What hinders you from
trusting fully in God's faithfulness?

Night Prayer

Lord, may you be
ever in my thoughts and prayers.
Keep me mindful of God
in the midst of my busy day.
Be my solace
as I lie in my bed at night.
For I know you are with me always,
ready to aid and give comfort.

Day Fifteen

◆◆◆◆◆

My Day Begins

Lord, you have been our dwelling place
in all generations.
Before the mountains were brought forth,
or ever you formed the earth and the world,
from everlasting to everlasting you are God.
You turn us back to the dust,
and say, "Turn back, O children of earth!"
For a thousand years in your sight

are but as yesterday when it is past,
or as a watch in the night.
You sweep us away; we are like a dream,
like grass which is renewed in the morning.
In the morning it flourishes and is renewed;
in the evening it fades and withers.
You have set our iniquities before you,
our secret sins in the light of your countenance.
For all our days pass away under your wrath,
our years come to an end like a sigh.
The years of our life are three score and ten,
or even by reason of strength fourscore;
yet their span is but toil and trouble;
they are soon gone, and we fly away.
So teach us to number our days

that we may get a heart of wisdom.
Return, O Lord! How long?
Have pity on your servants!
Satisfy us in the morning with your steadfast love,
that we may rejoice and be glad all our days.
Let your work be manifest to your servants,
and your glorious power to their children.
Establish the work of our hands,
yes, establish the work of our hands.

All Through the Day

Establish the work of our hands.

My Day Is Ending

Take a moment to sink into quiet
and relaxation. Follow your breathing.
Now reflect upon the
impermanence of life.
Look back at your past—
events, people, feelings.
How have they changed,
passed away, become only memories?

Put your hope and trust in God to sustain you.

Night Prayer

Lord, I thank you for this day
and all that it has brought me.
Help me to give thanks for it
and to let it go into your care.
I know you will be with me
all the days of my life.
I look forward to serving you tomorrow,
whatever you choose to give me then.

Day Sixteen

My Day Begins

Praise is due to you, O God, in Zion;
to you shall vows be performed,
O you who hear prayer.
Blessed is the one you choose and bring near
to dwell in your courts.
We shall be satisfied with the goodness
of your house, your holy temple.
Your strength established the mountains,

being girded with might.
You still the roaring of the seas,
the roaring of their waves,
the tumult of the peoples;
so that those who dwell at earth's farthest bounds
are afraid at your signs;
you make the outgoings of morning and evening
to shout for joy.
You visit the earth and water it,
you greatly enrich it;
the river of God is full of water.
You provide their grain,
for so you have prepared it.
You water its furrows abundantly,
settling its ridges, softening it with showers,

and blessing its growth.
You crown the year with your bounty.
The pastures of the wilderness drip,
the hills gird themselves with joy,
the meadows clothe themselves with flocks,
the valleys deck themselves with grain,
they shout and sing together for joy.

All Through the Day

Blessed is the one you choose
and bring near
to dwell in your courts!

My Day Is Ending

Spend a few minutes in quiet
and reflect over your day.
How did you remember
to praise God today?
How might you have
turned your mind to God
this day and given praise?

Night Prayer

Gracious Lord,
thank you for the glories
of your creation.
May they remind me of you
and your goodness to us.
Be with us through the night
and quicken our thoughts tomorrow.

Day Seventeen

◆◆◆◆◆

My Day Begins

Those who dwell in the shelter of the Most High,
who abide in the shadow of the Almighty,
will say to the Lord, "My refuge and my fortress;
my God, in whom I trust."
For God will deliver you from the snare of the fowler
and from the deadly pestilence.
With God's pinions you will be covered,
and under God's wings you will find refuge;

God's faithfulness is a shield and buckler.
You will not fear the terror of the night
nor the arrow that flies by day,
nor the pestilence that stalks in darkness,
nor the destruction that wastes at noonday.
You will only look with your eyes
and see the recompense of the wicked.
Because you have made the Lord your refuge,
the Most High your habitation,
no evil shall befall you,
no scourge come near your tent.
For God will put angels in charge of you
to guard you in all your ways.
On their hands they will bear you up,
lest you dash your foot against a stone.

YOU SHALL NOT WANT

You will tread on the lion and the adder.
Because you cleave to me in love,
I will deliver you;
I will protect you, because you know my name.
When you call to me, I will answer you;
I will be with you in trouble,
I will rescue you and honor you.
With long life I will satisfy you
and show you my salvation.

All Through the Day

Because you cleave to me in love,
I will deliver you.

My Day Is Ending

Take a few moments to look back
on your day.
How did you feel God's presence
and protection today?
Were there times when
you called out to God?
Might there have been
such opportunities?

Night Prayer

Lord, my protector,
watch over me through the night.
Keep me close to you,
guard me with your angels.
May all be safe
in the shadow of your wings.

Day Eighteen

My Day Begins

The Lord is my light and my salvation;
whom shall I fear?
The Lord is the stronghold of my life;
of whom shall I be afraid?
One thing have I asked of the Lord,
that will I seek after:
that I may dwell in the house of the Lord
all the days of my life,

to behold the beauty of the Lord,
and to inquire in God's temple.
For God will hide me in a shelter
in the day of trouble;
God will conceal me under the cover of the tent,
the Lord will set me high upon a rock.
And now my head shall be lifted up
above my enemies round about me;
I will offer in God's tent
sacrifices with shouts of joy;
I will sing and make melody to the Lord.
Hear, O Lord, when I cry aloud;
be gracious to me and answer me.
You have said, "Seek out my face."
My heart says to you,

"Your face, Lord, do I seek."
Hide not your face from me.
For my father and my mother have forsaken me,
but the Lord will take me up.
I believe that I shall see the goodness of the Lord
in the land of the living.
Wait for the Lord;
be strong and let your heart take courage;
yes, wait for the Lord.

All Through the Day

I ask to dwell
in the house of the Lord
all the days of my life.

My Day Is Ending

Spend a few minutes in quiet reflection.
Follow your breathing
as a way to center yourself in prayer.
How has God been your help today?
Where have you felt God's absence?
Where has God been especially present?

Night Prayer

Lord God,
hear me when I call upon you.
Do not let me
stray far from you.
Be with me in my weakness,
and I will praise you in my strength.

Day Nineteen

My Day Begins

Hear my prayer, O Lord;
give ear to my supplications.
In faithfulness answer me, in your righteousness.
Enter not into judgment with your servant;
for no living being is righteous before you.
For the enemy has pursued me
and crushed my life to the ground.

Therefore my spirit faints within me;
my heart within me is appalled.
I remember the days of old;
I meditate on all that you have done;
I muse on what your hands have wrought.
I stretch out my hands to you;
my soul thirsts for you like a parched land.
Make haste to answer me, O Lord!
My spirit fails!
Hide not your face from me,
lest I be like those who go down to the pit.
Let me hear in the morning of your steadfast love,
for in you I put my trust.
Teach me the way I should go,
for to you I lift up my soul.

Deliver me, O Lord, from my enemies!
I have fled to you for refuge!
Teach me to do your will,
for you are my God.
Let your good spirit lead me
on a level path.
For your name's sake, O Lord, preserve my life.
In your righteousness bring me out of trouble.
And in your steadfast love cut off my enemies,
for I am your servant.

All Through the Day

My soul thirsts for you
like a parched land.

My Day Is Ending

Take a few minutes now to review your day.
How has God been in your thoughts today?
Have you needed to call on God for help?
Would you do so should the need arise?
What would prevent you
from calling out?
What might help you to trust in God?

Night Prayer

Lord, I cry out to you;
be my safety, my stronghold.
Help me entrust myself to you
in my weakness.
Be my strength,
my rock, my God.

YOU SHALL NOT WANT

Day Twenty

◆◆◆◆◆

My Day Begins

I love the Lord, because God has heard
my voice and my supplications.
Because God has listened to me,
therefore I will call on the Lord as long as I live.
Gracious is the Lord, and righteous;
our God is merciful.
The Lord preserves the simple;
when I was brought low, the Lord saved me.

Return, O my soul, to your rest,
for the Lord has dealt bountifully with you.
You have delivered my soul from death,
my eyes from tears, my feet from stumbling;
I walk before the Lord in the land of the living.
I kept my faith, even when I said,
"I am greatly afflicted."
What shall I render to the Lord
for all God's bounty to me?
I will lift up the cup of salvation
and call on the name of the Lord;
I will pay my vows to the Lord
in the presence of all God's people.
O Lord, I am your servant;
you have loosed my bonds.

I will offer to you the sacrifice of thanksgiving
and call on the name of the Lord.
I will pay my vows to the Lord
in the presence of all the people,
in the courts of the house of the Lord,
in your midst, O Jerusalem.
Praise the Lord!

All Through the Day

Rest, O my soul,
for the Lord has dealt
bountifully with you.

My Day Is Ending

Pause for a few moments now
and reflect upon your day.
What moved you to call out to God?
When did you sense God's presence with you?
Are there times when you feel
close to God? Times when you feel removed?

Night Prayer

Lord, I cry out to you,
you are my guide,
my strength, my shield.
I will sing songs for you
in the presence of your people.
I will let all know of your love
and your wonderful deeds.

Day Twenty-One

◆◆◆◆◆

My Day Begins

Make a joyful noise to the Lord, all the earth;
sing the glory of God's name;
give to God glorious praise!
Say to God, "How awesome are your deeds;
all the earth worships you;
creation sings praises to you."
Come and see what God has done:
God turned the sea into dry land;

people passed through the river on foot.
There did we rejoice in the Lord,
who rules by might forever,
whose eyes keep watch on the nations—
let not the rebellious exalt themselves.
Bless our God, O peoples,
let the sound of God's praise be heard,
who has kept us among the living
and has not let our feet slip.
We went through fire and through water,
yet you have brought us forth to a spacious place.
I will come into your house with burnt offerings;
I will pay you my vows,
that which my lips uttered
and my mouth promised when I was in trouble.

You Shall Not Want

Come and hear, all you who fear God,
and I will tell what the Lord has done for me.
If I had cherished iniquity in my heart,
the Lord would not have listened.
But truly God has listened
and has given heed to the voice of my prayer.
Blessed be God,
who has not rejected my prayer
nor removed God's steadfast love from me!

All Through the Day

You have brought us forth
to a spacious place.

My Day Is Ending

Spend a few minutes tonight
reflecting upon those things
God has done for you, your family,
your community, your country.
How has God shown care for you?
Take some time to give thanks to God.

Night Prayer

Gracious Lord,
you have been our protector
and our strength.
Thank you for all your blessings—
in my life and in our land.
I will sing your praise forever.
And may we dwell in peace.

Day Twenty-Two

◆◆◆◆◆

My Day Begins

How lovely is your dwelling place,
O Lord of hosts!
My soul longs, yea, faints for the courts of the Lord;
my heart and flesh sing for joy to the living God.
Even the sparrow finds a home,
and the swallow a nest for herself,
where she may lay her young at your altar.
Blessed are those whose strength is in you,

in whose heart are the highways to Zion.
As they go through the valley of Baca
they make it a place of springs;
the early rain also covers it with pools.
They go from strength to strength;
the God of gods will be seen in Zion.
For a day in your courts is better
than a thousand elsewhere.
I would rather be a doorkeeper in the house of God
than dwell in the tents of wickedness.
For the Lord God is a sun and shield,
bestowing favor and honor.
No good thing will the Lord withhold
from them who walk uprightly.

May our sons in their youth
be like plants full grown,
our daughters like corner pillars
cut for the structure of a palace.
May our granaries be full,
providing all manner of store.
May our cattle be heavy with young,
suffering no mischance or failure in bearing.
May there be no cry of distress in our streets.
Happy the people to whom such blessings fall!
Happy the people whose God is the Lord!

All Through the Day

A day in your courts
is better
than a thousand elsewhere.

My Day Is Ending

Take some time simply to dwell
in the Lord.
Repeat the phrase
from today to help you
stay centered.
Or reflect upon
God's blessings you have received.

Night Prayer

Lord, it is good to be with you.
I am happy to dwell
in your presence.
I ask your blessings
upon myself, my family,
and my community.
May we welcome all
in your name
and show them your grace.

Day Twenty-Three

◆◆◆◆◆

My Day Begins

Out of the depths I cry to you, O Lord.
Lord, hear my voice.
Let your ears be attentive
to the voice of my supplications.
If you, O Lord, should mark iniquities,
Lord, who could stand?
But there is forgiveness with you,
that you may be feared.

I wait for the Lord, my soul waits,
and in God's word I hope.
My soul waits for the Lord
more than those who watch for the morning,
yes, more than those who watch for the morning.
O Israel, hope in the Lord;
for with the Lord there is steadfast love,
and in God is found plenteous redemption.
And God will redeem Israel
from all iniquities.

I cry with my voice to the Lord,
with my voice I make supplication to the Lord,
I pour out my complaint before God;
I tell my trouble before God.

When my spirit is faint,
you know my way.
Deliver me from my persecutors;
for they are too strong for me.
Bring me out of prison,
that I may give thanks to your name.
The righteous will surround me;
for you will deal bountifully with me.

All Through the Day

With the Lord there is steadfast love.

My Day Is Ending

Perhaps you
are not in the position of the
one who laments in today's psalm,
but many people are.
Take some time now to call them to mind
and include them in your prayer.

Night Prayer

Lord, be my comfort and strength.
Draw into your care
all those who are suffering.
Show them your support
and love.
Help me to be a source
of care and love for all who suffer.

Day Twenty-Four

My Day Begins

Praise the Lord!
Praise the Lord, O my soul!
I will praise the Lord as long as I live;
I will sing praises to my God while I have being.
Happy are we whose help is the God of Rachel and Jacob,
whose hope is in the Lord our God,
who made heaven and earth,
the sea, and all that is in them;

who keeps faith forever,
who executes justice for the oppressed,
who gives food to the hungry.
The Lord sets the prisoners free;
The Lord opens the eyes of the blind.
The Lord lifts up those who are bowed down;
the Lord loves the righteous.
The Lord watches over the immigrants,
and upholds the widow and the orphan.

Praise the Lord!
It is good to sing praises to our God,
for God is gracious, and a song of praise is seemly.
The Lord builds up Jerusalem,
and gathers the outcasts of Israel.
God heals the brokenhearted,

and binds up their wounds.
The Lord determines the number of the stars,
and gives to all of them their names.
Great is our Lord, and abundant in power;
God's understanding is beyond measure.
Sing to the Lord with thanksgiving,
make melody to our God upon the lyre!
God covers the heavens with clouds
and prepares rain for the earth,
making grass grow upon the hills.
God gives animals their food,
and feeds the young ravens who cry out.
The Lord takes pleasure in those who do reverence,
in those who hope in God's steadfast love.

◆◆◆◆

All Through the Day

God's understanding is beyond measure.

My Day Is Ending

Take a few minutes now
and reflect upon
which images of creation
speak to you about God.
The psalm mentions the heavens and the sun.
Which creatures reveal God to you?
The psalm also mentions
God's concern for the poor and marginal.
How does this fit with your image of God?
How might you show God's concern
for those in trouble?

Night Prayer

Lord, all creation
speaks to me of your love and glory.
May I show forth your love and compassion
to all who are oppressed
and in trouble.
Let me be a sign of your mercy
to all people.

Day Twenty-Five

My Day Begins

It is good to give thanks to the Lord,
to sing praises to your name, O Most High,
to declare your steadfast love in the morning,
and your faithfulness by night,
to the music of the lute and the harp,
to the melody of the lyre.
For you, O Lord, have made me glad by your work.
At the works of your hands I sing for joy.

How great are your works, O Lord!
Your thoughts are very deep.
The dull cannot know,
the stupid cannot understand this;
that, though the wicked sprout like grass
and all evildoers flourish,
they are doomed to destruction forever,
but you, O Lord, are on high forever.
For, lo, your enemies, O Lord,
for, lo, your enemies shall perish;
all evildoers shall be scattered.
But you have exalted my horn like the wild ox;
you have poured over me fresh oil.
My eyes have seen the downfall of my enemies,
my ears have heard the doom of my evil assailants.

The righteous flourish like the palm tree,
and grow like a cedar in Lebanon.
They are planted in the house of the Lord;
they flourish in the courts of our God.
They still bring forth fruit in old age;
they are ever full of sap and green,
to show that the Lord is upright.
God is my rock,
and there is no unrighteousness in the Lord.

All Through the Day

At the works of your hands I sing for joy.

You Shall Not Want

My Day Is Ending

The image of the
flourishing plant is found in this psalm.
Remain with this image for a time.
Read over the lines in the psalm
to help you expand it.
Don't try to analyze;
let the image reveal itself.

Night Prayer

Lord, as I see the green of your world,
I feel your glory and vitality.
In your ways I flourish,
and by your paths
I walk in the way of life.
Thank you for all the blessings
you have given me.

Day Twenty-Six

◆◆◆◆◆

My Day Begins

Not to us, O Lord, not to us,
but to your name give glory
for the sake of your steadfast love and faithfulness.
Why should the nations say, "Where is their God?"
Our God is in the heavens, and does what is pleasing.
Their idols are silver and gold,
the work of human hands.
They have ears, but do not hear;

noses, but do not smell.
They do not make a sound in their throat.
Those who make them are like them;
so are all who trust in them.

O Israel, trust in the Lord!
God is your help and your shield.
O house of Aaron, put your trust in the Lord.
God is your help and your shield.
You who fear the Lord, trust in the Lord.
God is your help and your shield.
The Lord has been mindful of us; God will bless us;
God will bless those who fear the Lord,
both small and great.
May the Lord give you increase,
you and your children.

May you be blessed by the Lord,
who made heaven and earth.
The heavens are the Lord's heavens,
but the earth God has given to us.
The dead do not praise the Lord
nor do any that go down into silence.
But we will bless the Lord
from this time forth and forevermore.
Praise the Lord!

All Through the Day

The earth God has given to us.

YOU SHALL NOT WANT

My Day Is Ending

The psalm speaks of idols.
Today we still worship or
idolize things that are less than God.
Can you see what idols may
be functioning in your own life?
Power? Success? Addiction? Control?
Ask God to remove them for you.

Night Prayer

Lord, help me to leave behind
all that is not of you.
Enlighten me to the idols
in my life,
and help me leave them behind.
I want you as my sole foundation.

Day Twenty-Seven

◆◆◆◆◆

My Day Begins

O Lord, you have searched me and known me.
You know when I sit down and when I rise up;
you discern my thoughts from afar.
You search out my path and my lying down,
and you are acquainted with all my ways—
even before a word is on my tongue.
Such knowledge is too wonderful for me;
it is high, and I cannot attain it.

Where shall I hide from your Spirit?
If I take the wings of the morning
and dwell in the uttermost parts of the sea,
even there your hand shall lead me,
and your right hand shall hold me.
If I say, "Let only darkness cover me,
and the light about me be night,"
even the darkness is not dark to you;
the night is bright as the day,
for darkness is as light with you.
For you formed my inner parts;
you knit me together in my mother's womb.
Your eyes beheld my unformed substance.
In your book were written, every one of them,
the days that were formed for me,

when as yet there was none of them.
How precious to me are your thoughts, O God.
How vast is the sum of them.
If I would count them, they are more than the sand.
When I awake, I am still with you.
Search me, O God, and know my heart.
Try me and know my thoughts.
See if there is any wickedness in me,
and lead me in the way everlasting.

All Through the Day

Search me, God, and know my thoughts.

You Shall Not Want

My Day Is Ending

Today's psalm prayer praises God
for God's infinite knowledge.
Awe and wonder are essential
components of the religious experience.

Spend a few minutes now
in contemplation.
What arouses your own awe and wonder?
The heavens? The human mystery?
Beauty? Nature? Community? Love?

Night Prayer

Lord, you know me
better than I know myself.
Guide my steps in your ways.
Help me to grow in wisdom.

Day Twenty-Eight

My Day Begins

Come, bless the Lord,
all you servants of the Lord,
who stand by night in the house of the Lord.
Lift up your hands to the holy place
and bless the Lord.
May the Lord bless you from Zion,
God, who made heaven and earth.
Praise the Lord!

Praise the name of the Lord,
give praise, O servants of the Lord,
you that stand in the house of the Lord,
in the courts of the house of our God.
For I know that the Lord is great,
and that our Lord is above all gods.
God makes the clouds rise at the end of the earth,
and makes lightning for the rain
and brings forth the wind from the storehouses.
God it was who in your midst, O Egypt,
sent signs and wonders
against Pharaoh and all his servants.
God it was who smote many nations
and gave their land as a heritage,
a heritage to our people Israel.

You Shall Not Want

Your name, O Lord, endures forever,
your renown, O Lord, throughout all ages.
For the Lord will vindicate the people
and have compassion on God's servants.
O house of Israel, bless the Lord!
You that fear the Lord, bless the Lord!
Blessed be the Lord from Zion,
the God who dwells in Jerusalem.
Praise the Lord!

All Through the Day

Let us lift up our hands
to the holy place
and bless the Lord.

My Day Is Ending

The psalm prayer recounts
the history of Israel's
liberation from Egypt.
Spend some time now
reflecting on your own experience
of liberation.
From what have you been set free?
From what do you still seek liberation?

Night Prayer

Bless you, my God,
for the wonders of your world.
I praise you for your great acts,
which lift up the downtrodden
and liberate those held prisoner.
Lift my burdens and those of my neighbors
so that we may enjoy
your peace and your favor.

Day Twenty-Nine

My Day Begins

My God, my God, why have you forsaken me?
Why are you so far from helping me,
from the words of my groaning?
O my God, I cry by day, but you do not answer,
and by night, but find no rest.
Yet you are holy,
enthroned on the praises of Israel.

In you our ancestors trusted;
they trusted, and you delivered them.
But I am a worm, not human,
scorned by all, and despised by the people.
All who see me, mock me;
they make faces at me and wag their heads.
"He committed his cause to God; let God deliver him."
Yet it was you who took me from the womb;
you kept me safe upon my mother's breasts.
Be not far from me, for trouble is near
and there is none to help.
I am poured out like water,
and all my bones are out of joint.
My heart is like wax;
it is melted within my breast.

YOU SHALL NOT WANT

You lay me in the dust of death.
A company of evildoers encircles me;
they have pierced my hands and feet—
they divide my garments among them,
and for my raiment they cast lots.
But you, O Lord, be not far off.
I will tell of your name to my family;
in the midst of the congregation I will praise you.
All the ends of the earth shall remember
and turn to the Lord.

All Through the Day

They trusted and you delivered them.

YOU SHALL NOT WANT

My Day Is Ending

This psalm prayer plumbs the depths
of despair,
yet affirms faith and trust
that God will come to the rescue.

How does this psalm relate
to your own faith and experience?
Do you cry out to God in times of despair?
Do you have faith that God will see you through?

Night Prayer

Lord, may I turn to you
for comfort in times of pain and sorrow?
Help me to trust in your care
and to have faith that you
will never abandon me to destruction.

Day Thirty

My Day Begins

Praise the Lord!
Praise the Lord from the heavens;
praise God in the heights.
Praise the Lord, all angels;
praise God, all the heavenly host.
Praise God, sun and moon;
praise God, all you shining stars.
Praise God, you highest heavens

and you waters above the heavens.
Let them praise the name of the Lord.
For God commanded and they were created.
Praise the Lord from the earth,
you fire and hail, snow and frost,
stormy wind fulfilling God's command,
mountains and all hills, fruit trees and all cedars,
beasts and all cattle, creeping and flying creatures,
young men and maidens together,
old people and children.
Let them praise the name of the Lord,
for God's name alone is exalted;
God's glory is above earth and heaven.
Sing to the Lord a new song,
sing praise in the assembly of the faithful.

YOU SHALL NOT WANT

Let Israel be glad in its Maker;
let the children of Zion rejoice in their King.
Let them praise God's name with dancing,
making melody to the Lord with timbrel and lyre.
For the Lord takes pleasure in the people;
and adorns the humble with victory.
Let everything that breathes praise the Lord.
Praise the Lord!

All Through the Day

The Lord takes pleasure in the people.

My Day Is Ending

Take a few minutes to reflect
on the things that raise your soul
to praise God.
How do you experience the wonder of God?

Name aloud some of these experiences
as today's psalm does.
Make your own psalm of praise to God.

Night Prayer

Lord, all your works
show your glory.
I stand in wonder
when I behold them.
I join in the chorus of all creation,
sun and stars, animals and humans,
as we all sing your praises and give thanks
for your generosity and love.

One Final Word

This book was created to be nothing more than a gateway—a gateway to the spiritual wisdom of a specific tradition of prayer, a gateway opening on your own spiritual path.

You may decide that the psalms are a form of prayer that provide an experience of God that you wish to explore more closely and deeply. In that case you should find a translation of their entire text that you find readable. Put it at your bedside; carry it with you. Pray it as you have prayed this journey.

You may, however, decide that the form of prayer represented by the psalms does not come easily to you. Do not abandon it too easily or too quickly, but also do not feel guilty. There are many other teachers, many other traditions, and many other forms of prayer. Somewhere there is the right one for your very special and absolutely unique journey of the spirit. What works for you today may not come easily tomorrow. The reverse is also true. Do not force the issue. Go where the spirit leads you. You will find your teacher and you will discover your path.

We would not be searching, as St. Augustine reminds us, if we had not already been found.

One more thing should be said: Spirituality is not meant to be self-absorption, a cocoonish relationship of "God and me." In the long run, if it is to have meaning, if it is to grow and not wither, it must be a wellspring of compassionate living. It must reach out to others as God has reached out to us.

True spirituality breaks down the walls of our souls and lets in not just heaven, but the whole world.